To Jay, with deep appreciation for
your willingness to serve as a
mentor. College Mennonite Church
July 31, 1994

When a
Teenager
Chooses
You—

When a Teenager Chooses You—

as Friend, Confidante, Confirmation Sponsor

Practical Advice for Any Adult

Joseph Moore

Nihil Obstat: Rev. Hilarion Kistner, O.F.M.
Rev. John J. Jennings
Rev. Edward Gratsch

Imprimi Potest: Rev. Jeremy Harrington, O.F.M.
Provincial

Imprimatur: +James H. Garland, V.G.
Archdiocese of Cincinnati
March 5, 1987; May 3, 1989

The *nihil obstat* and *imprimatur* are a declaration that a book is considered to be free from doctrinal or moral error. It is not implied that those who have granted the *nihil obstat* and *imprimatur* agree with the contents, opinions or statements expressed.

Scripture citations are taken from the *New American Bible*, copyright © 1970 by the Confraternity of Christian Doctrine, Washington, D.C., and are used by permission of the copyright owner. All rights reserved.

The "Litany of the Holy Spirit" is reprinted from *CHOICE* by Joseph Moore, © 1986 by Joseph Moore, and is used by permission of Paulist Press.

Cover and book design by Robert Roose

Contents

For Darrell Smith,
peer minister par excellence

Introduction

Accepting the Challenge

You probably never imagined yourself as a "mentor." But suddenly you find yourself in the role of "spiritual guide" for a teenager. Perhaps you have been asked to be a sponsor at Confirmation—a role which is becoming increasingly meaningful. Or maybe your own child's friends or some young relative considers you someone with whom a youngster can talk about personal issues and faith. Or maybe you work with the high school CCD program or parish youth group.

Your "mentoring" may be short-term—a couple of significant conversations over a particular issue or a now-and-then encounter as the young person's needs emerge. Or you may be meeting with a teenager on a very regular and structured basis as in a Confirmation program. Whatever the context, this book is for you.

Religious educator Dolores Curran says that every adolescent needs a "special adult" to talk with—someone other than parents, someone who won't judge or worry or repeat later what he or she said. Thinking back on your own youth, you may recall some person who fulfilled this role for you. Something attracts young people to certain adults and enables them to express confidential matters. If a young person has chosen you, graciously accept that fact and realize that you have something very special to offer.

It's not hard to tell you've been chosen. A teenager begins hanging around your kitchen to continue a conversation or says something like, "I wish I could talk to my folks like I talk with you." These are examples of the many subtle clues that indicate young people feel comfortable talking with you and that there is more they would like to say. Often they don't even know specifically what that "more" is. They just want to put their hopes, fears and questions into words with a trusted adult who does not have parental authority over them.

Spirituality includes *all* our deeper concerns— concerns about life's meaning, our identity, relationships and, of course, the place of God in human life. So a "spiritual guide" is not someone who only talks about prayer with a young person. We are referring to an adult who takes an interest in a teenager's inner journey, the struggle to grow into maturity.

Spiritual direction is a very precise term which defines the role of a person offering support, encouragement and (sometimes) advice to another who is seeking a deeper relationship with the Lord. Spiritual direction properly occurs among adults (and is to be distinguished from psychological counseling which also has a great role to play in total human development). Adults can focus just on their spiritual growth because they have already achieved emotional maturity—at least to a large degree.

Young people, on the other hand, are not yet

emotionally mature. Thus their "spiritual life" is bound up with their continuing emotional development. That is the reason for the term *spiritual guide* (rather than spiritual director) to label the adult who is called upon to assist a teenager's religious development, and that is why this book addresses issues of human development as well as spirituality.

Chapter One describes teenagers in the contemporary world. Their culture is very different from the teen culture of 20 years ago. Their music and dress styles are enough to scare some adults. It is a different world, admittedly, but kids are still kids and have all the same fears and hopes we had growing up. Chapter Two discusses just why *you* are qualified to be of help to a young person and offers some pointers about being a good listener.

Chapter Three, the heart of the book, offers concrete suggestions for guiding a youngster in prayer and spirituality. Chapter Four explores the realm of morality with some practical suggestions for helping with critical issues, but offers no magic formula or specific program. Next you will find a list of Gospel passages for shared reflection as well as a helpful bibliography.

The final section is for those of you who are responsible for setting up formal Confirmation programs in your parish. This section presents four options for Confirmation preparation programs: (1) a meeting for sponsors, (2) a three- to four-hour mini-retreat for candidates and sponsors, (3) an unstructured, one-on-one program for candidates and sponsors, (4) an outline of a structured four-week, one-on-one program for candidates and sponsors.

The teenager who has approached you for spiritual guidance perceives you as someone who has something to offer. Trust that perception and turn to God for the graces you will need in the adventuresome walk with a young person on a spiritual journey.

Chapter
1

What Makes
a Teenager 'Tick'?

We can all remember certain aspects of our lives as teenagers—perhaps times of either intense happiness or great unhappiness. But most of us quickly forgot a lot of what it feels like to be a teenager. And, of course, we were teens within a culture quite different from today's. And so we will begin by talking about what's going on within young people, what makes them "tick."

Searching for Identity

Psychologists tell us that we all pass through crucial stages between birth and adolescence. During adolescence young people begin to deal with the question: "Who am I *really*?" It's a time of defining their unique personalities and what they want to become. But during this process teenagers will probably experience some degree of "identity confusion": isolation, emptiness, anxiety and indecisiveness.

They feel the need to make significant life choices; yet, at the same time, they feel unable to do so. They also feel that society and adults are pushing them toward decisions. As a result they can easily become resistant. This is when a retreat to childhood appears as a pleasant alternative to the world of adult pressures.

Understandably, behavior can be pretty inconsistent and unpredictable during this period. At one minute the teenager doesn't want to make a commitment to anyone or anything—and the very next minute is willing to follow some cause or person no matter the consequences.

For adults this can be a very trying time unless we understand what's going on. We almost have to brace ourselves to *expect* this vacillation, this very contradictory behavior. We need to recognize it as normal and necessary and try not to take it too personally when we suffer because of it. We need some detachment from the inner storm of teenagers, otherwise we can easily be swept into turmoil ourselves. And then we aren't good for ourselves or for them.

Because this task of discovering "who I am" is a scary one calling for openness and intimacy, some teenagers use avoidance techniques—what psychologists call "defenses." Some common defenses include: frequent partying or distractions; using alcohol, marijuana or cocaine, *excessive* absorption in television (perhaps MTV, the music channel); taking on a "role" (macho, athlete, scholar, clown, preppie) rather than discovering who they really are; indulging in sexual behavior; living in the "fast lane," always "on the go"; adopting a value structure opposed to authority and adults, thereby assuming a negative identity.

These avoidance techniques take the pressure off genuine self-discovery. Unfortunately they also tend to reinforce and aggravate the present state of confusion. As adults we need to point out to young people the behavior we observe and challenge them to confront the crucial task of identity formation.

During this time of identity crisis we need to be understanding—and yet we need to be ourselves and stick to our own tasks and life choices. We can be most helpful by being good listeners. (We'll talk more about listening in Chapter Two.) We're even more helpful when we don't listen judgmentally, but allow young people to come to their own decisions—temporary as they may be. (Of course this is much easier for adults who are *not* their parents.)

For example, I once had a boy come to me and ask my advice about having sexual intercourse on the night of his junior prom. My first temptation was to scream, "Don't!"

But I caught myself when I realized that he had obviously chosen me because he felt safe enough with me to discuss this very personal matter. He also probably was feeling ambivalent about the prospect and was clearly looking for some adult guidance. But if I immediately moralized or yelled at him or made a pronouncement, he would probably pay little attention to what I had to say.

So I bit my tongue. I listened patiently and as nonjudgmentally as possible to all the pros and cons he presented. In this way I was able to reinforce all his own negative feelings about such an action and to support him in his struggle to live a moral Christian life simply by agreeing with the objections he himself was presenting.

When he was all through speaking, *then* I was able to tell him that I thought he knew the right thing to do, that I knew him and believed his deep-down values were good. I think that at his deepest level he knew that to have sex would be wrong and harmful to this relationship and also against the wise teachings of the Church. I was confident he would do the moral thing and I admitted I felt honored that he had trusted me with this very personal matter.

This is what I mean by nonjudgmental listening. Teenagers need to talk about themselves, reveal themselves and their private thoughts to others, especially their peers. By opening up and talking honestly about what they are feeling and thinking, young people develop the capacity called *intimacy*. And it's intimacy—openness, vulnerability—that eventually solidifies human identities. This is how we discover and become who we truly are: through the lifelong process of revealing ourselves.

Moving Toward Independence

Sooner or later the adolescent begins to withdraw emotionally from the parental relationship. This necessary move toward adulthood is both exciting and painful for the teenager—and can also be painful for parents. Consider these two reports from a mother and her teenage son.

First, from the mother:

I'm having a tough time, a real tough time, in letting my oldest son go. I mean it's really hard. He's still my little boy, my baby. I carried him within me. I nursed and nourished him and have been devoted to his every need along the way. And now he wants to break away from me and I can't bear it.

He runs from me. He darts away from all the time I'd like to spend with him. I think he feels smothered by my love. Well, it isn't really love. It's not making him feel free. He feels caged. No it's not love; it's my need to hang on to him. And I'm jealous too of other people to whom he turns to share his deepest secrets. He used to share them all with me. I feel very alone.

Then, from the son:

You see, my mother—she just doesn't understand. I love her so much, more than anything. But she doesn't think I do because I don't spend any time with her and with our family. I don't know. I just have to be on the go. I find it hard to spend time at home and I'd rather be with my friends.

Do you think I'm wrong? Sometimes I do—when I can see a lonely, hurt look in my mother's eyes as I'm leaving the house. I feel guilty. I guess I'm pretty selfish about it. Adults like companionship and closeness just as much as I do. I want my family there when *I* feel the need, but most of the time I ignore *their* needs. I never think about making them happy. I'm so wrapped up in making myself happy. I wish I could tell this to my mother when she looks at me that way.

If we don't recognize this very natural struggle for independence, we will become irritated, hurt or exasperated in our relationships with young people.

Take, for example, the issue of a teenager's friends. During childhood, children pretty much take for granted their parents' judgments about who are "nice people" and who are not. Teenagers may question these judgments and strike up friendships with people of whom parents disapprove. This not only helps the adolescent attain some distance from the parents, but also provides a chance to weigh and test what was previously accepted without question. Yet parents may experience such an action as defying their authority. Or they fear for the teen who seems to be "running with the wrong crowd."

How does one respond to the situation as an adult offering guidance? The answer is not simple, but here are some suggestions for dealing with this phenomenon:

- •Perhaps *most* importantly, try to understand what is going on inside the teenager struggling to become his or her own person.
- •Don't "put down" friends, but ask what the teenager looks for in a friendship, what values it represents. In other words, help the youngster to reflect on the choices being made.
- •Act as a bridge between parent and child. Point out that while you understand that we all want to be free to choose our own friends, parents want only the best for their children and have legitimate fears about the possibility of negative influences on a young person's life.
- •If you are asked directly what *you* think about the friend in question, answer honestly and directly. Young

people prize honesty in relationships perhaps more than anything else. If you are honest and open with teenagers they will be unable to have anything but respect for you even if they express total disagreement.

Erma Bombeck compares children to kites which parents spend a lifetime trying to get off the ground. The art of parenting can be compared to letting out the right amount of string as the adolescent grows and emerges into young adulthood. But seeing the "kite" rise higher and higher into the sky brings both sadness and joy. Parents know that it won't be long before that beautiful creature will snap the lifeline that once bound them together and soar as it was meant to, free and alone. Only then, Erma says, do parents know that they did their job.

As teenagers grow away from us, however, we adults have a lot of difficulty dealing with the event emotionally. This is most difficult for parents with their first teenager. Non-parents can often be more objective and encourage the reluctant adult in the art of "letting go." But non-parents can also have difficulty. Any adult who has become close to a child—a teacher, a friend, a minister—faces the temptation to try to keep the child dependent or to become overprotective or possessive because it is so painful to see the child withdraw.

What we need to realize is that our relationship with them is not "over" (even though it may appear that way for a while). The ground of the relationship is shifting, and that shifting is necessary if we ever want to reestablish ourselves in a new adult-to-adult relationship. If we try to repress or smother this natural development, we run the risk of alienating the young person from us forever. Reflect on these beautiful words from Kahlil Gibran's *The Prophet:*

> Your children are not your children.
> They are the sons and daughters of Life's longing for
> itself....
> You may give them your love but not your thoughts....
> You may house their bodies but not their souls....
> You are the bows from which your children as living

arrows are sent forth....
Let your bending in the archer's hand be for gladness....

During the transition to adulthood, the teenager finds a temporary "way station" among his or her peer group. There a young person finds a sense of belonging and a feeling of strength. In order to gain acceptance by the group, teenagers often tend to conform completely in dress, hairstyles, musical tastes, and so on. Young teens need the experience of acceptance by their peers in order to solidify their sense of self-esteem (see p. 25). Later in adolescence, however, they will need to individuate themselves from the group with a new appreciation of their own uniqueness.

The telephone ("dial-a-peer") becomes very significant during this period of envelopment by the group. Psychiatrists have suggested that the phone provides the teen with a wonderful means of flight from parents to peers without ever leaving home. It also provides opportunity for a romantic—even erotic—closeness with a member of the opposite sex while maintaining a safe physical distance.

Another very significant "peer connector" is music. Teens live surrounded by music, even more so today since the advent of the cable music channel, MTV. Both the music itself and the dancing it engenders satisfy a number of needs for teenagers. Music is one of the "languages" or common denominators of the peer group. Delight in the physical movement of dance offers a feeling of release from tensions. Dance also provides a means of expressing both sexual urges (which are surging at this time in life) and aggression in a safe and symbolic way.

Dance forms today are admittedly much freer in body movement than those of our youth, but we should not be too quick to label the gyrations immodest. The whole cultural view of sexuality with which our young people have grown up is quite different from the society in which most of us were teenagers. If the way teenagers dance today bothers you, the best advice is this: Never volunteer to chaperone!

Riding an Emotional Rollercoaster

Teens are subject to frequent mood swings. One recent study concludes that a mood of extreme happiness or extreme sadness lasts, on average, about 45 minutes. Yet we all know how such short-lived moods can impact those surrounding the adolescent!

Environment has a lot to do with mood swings in young people. The teenager in school may seem to be a different person from the one coming home with friends. Some people theorize that puberty, the biological changes occurring within the young teenager, increases the base level of hormones. This requires various adjustments in the body which, in turn, cause mood swings.

Others think that the emotional breaking away from parents causes a sort of "mourning" or depression. As a counter-reaction moods of elation occur when *new* love objects are found. In other words, the mood swings of teenagers are related to the making or breaking of relationships either in reality or in their fantasy life. Still others say that adolescents are pressured to take on the responsibilities of adulthood, and at the same time, they are supposed to enjoy the pleasures of youth—and that this double expectation causes moodiness.

Whatever the cause of mood swings, the important issue is how teenagers handle them. And we can help them by getting the youngster to talk about whatever has him or her in its grip. When a kid approaches you in a "down" mood just ask, "How come so blue?" Talking about it will make the teen feel at least 50 percent better.

Sometimes teens don't understand why they are feeling depressed, but they should still be encouraged to talk. That in itself may provide the key to understanding and lead to a lifting of the "heavy" feelings.

Those young people who learn to control their energies and, despite their moods, move toward their goals in life will become confident individuals. Mood swings need to be recognized as challenges: The junior in high school who wants good grades in order to be accepted by the chosen college needs to study and perform even though he or she may not feel like it at any given time. Doing so brings a self-satisfaction which will reinforce the ability to take charge of life. Our place as adults is on the sidelines because young people have to do this for themselves. But our role on the sidelines is not to nag them, but rather to cheer them on with the proper doses of encouragement and support.

Life has given all of us hard lessons in maturity. We have struggled ourselves in delaying gratification in order to attain some distant goal or preserve some value. We have all put aside our moods and made sacrifices at home and at work. This is the task we must teach teenagers to begin.

Psychology today has put a lot of emphasis on feeling—and rightly so. For too long society, and the Churches as well, have neglected the emotional part of life. But we also need to keep feelings in perspective. "If it feels good, do it" is not a formula for mature human or Christian behavior.

Moods will come and go. We need to help teens understand that the inner core of who they are as a person needs to be stronger than all these emotional ups and downs.

Along with the emotional turbulence, teens develop new reasoning skills. Around the age of 12, preteens begin to develop a greater capacity for thinking. For example, they can start to hypothesize ("what if..."), form generalizations and move from thinking in concrete terms to abstract thought. This expansion of the mind allows for the consideration of deeper questions: the meaning of life, God, personal values. But it also brings with it the question *Why?*

Adults can easily get exasperated when the young person who once accepted things readily now barrages them with "*Why* do I have to?" or "*Why* can't I?" "*Why* do I have to go to church?" "*Why* can't I bum around Europe?" It's easy for parents to lose patience with this type of interrogation or to view it as a challenge to their authority.

As teenagers grow older, it's important that caring adults take the time to discuss the "whys" that young people raise. This type of communication helps them to increase their mental powers and, more importantly, to get deeper insights into adult reasoning. Why do we as adults hold certain values precious? Why do parents think limits serve teenagers' own best interests?

We adults have more emotional detachment serving as guides for other people's children. We can listen more easily when we do not feel our own parental authority threatened. By absorbing some share of teenagers' negativity, we can provide a safe place for a young person to struggle toward independence.

Growing in Faith

Up to now we have been talking, for the most part, in psychological terms. Of course all these psychological factors have a bearing on spirituality and religious development. Before we begin a discussion of faith, however, we need to define terms.

When you were growing up, perhaps *faith* meant giving intellectual assent to the teaching of the Church. But today the word *faith* means something that involves the whole person, not just the head. It means relating to God in a way that invests energies, heart and hope.

When the Jewish Scriptures call Abraham the "man of *faith*," the Hebrew word is closer to our word *trust*. Faith is a trusting, a commitment to the belief that God cares for us and will bring us safely through eveything, including the curtain of death.

Adolescents are in the process of *growing* in faith. Research on the stages of faith indicates that young people between the ages of 12 and 20 are primarily concerned with relationships—the "interpersonal," we call it. This is the period when people learn intimacy and when true friendship becomes an important part of life. It's a time to learn to relate to people of the opposite sex in a romantic way. All teenagers make a lot of mistakes in exploring this whole realm of relationship, but that's necessary for continued growth as a person.

The religious faith of young people likewise involves the discovery that they are in *relationship* with God or Jesus Christ. They discover that God isn't someone up in the sky or in the Bible, but a real person who cares about them and who calls them to trust. Just as the development of a human relationship requires communication, so does a relationship with Jesus or God. We call this communication "prayer."

In the later Middle Ages, under the influence of St. Teresa of Avila and St. John of the Cross, faith growth was understood in terms of "stages in the spiritual life." These stages are worth discussing briefly because this part of our heritage still has something to offer today. These are the stages the great spiritual writers describe:

1) *Primitive Spirituality:* Prayer is basically *me*-centered with a "Gimme this, God" attitude. This is spiritual childhood.

2) *Purgative Stage:* We begin to get rid of false ideas and see God as a person, a friend with whom we are in relationship. Teenagers also begin to see parents and other adults as human beings and friends.

3) *Illuminative Stage:* We begin to realize that God accepts us totally for who we are, as we are. We begin to get rid of our low self-esteem and accept ourselves.

4) *The "Dark Night of the Soul":* We discover we can't control our feelings in prayer. Sometimes it is hard to pray and God seems absent. We begin to realize that feeling God's presence is a gift over which we have no control.

5) *Unitive Stage:* We realize that life and prayer are one and that God is within us constantly. In contemporary jargon, it is a feeling of inner freedom and being "together," connected to the universe.

Developing a Moral Sense

Linked to faith, of course, is moral development: how this relationship with Jesus Christ impacts life-style, attitudes, behavior. There have been even more studies on the stages of moral development than on the stages of faith development. A common opinion is that teenagers have not reached the moral maturity to choose the right thing consistently because their interior value system is not fully developed. Rather they are at a stage where they are very concerned about group expectations. Their behavior is often based upon what they feel others want them to do. This is not a bad place to be.

But as they get older, they need to develop their own inner convictions about what is right and wrong and act more from those convictions than from what others think. They also need to pass through a period when they begin to realize that moral issues can be very complex and that reflection is required (more on this when we talk about conscience, p. 42). Despite the ambiguity in many moral dilemmas, the older teenager will eventually need to connect personal meaning, commitment and responsibility to the choices he or she makes in life.

Another aspect of teenagers' moral development is that they are very self-absorbed and generally lack a very wide range of concern. "Do your own thing" is still a very popular adolescent attitude. They are extremely self-absorbed—which sometimes deludes young people into thinking that everyone else is as interested in them as they are! If you have ever watched one of them in front of a mirror getting ready for a date you know what I'm talking about. This self-absorption can be accompanied by a kind of mystique which allows teens to believe they can do nothing wrong, that nothing is ever their fault, that blame is never theirs. (Sound familiar?)

Certainly we need to point out that they can be at fault and that they are indeed responsible for the consequences of their behavior. At the same time it might help to remember that their cocoon of self-centeredness can make them unaware of the hurt they are causing others. One function of spiritual guidance is to help them realize when their behavior is negatively affecting others.

Needing Structure and Guidance

The present generation of parents are perhaps more ambivalent in their own values or concepts of right and wrong than parents before them. Uncertainty is not bad in itself, but teens usually interpret uncertainty as license. When adults say "I don't know" or "I'm not sure," teens often hear "I don't *care*." Our delicate task as spiritual guides is to weave our own values and beliefs into our discussions even when we must admit uncertainty.

Limits provide the security and structure young people need to discover who they are and what their own values are. Establishing those limits is, of course, the role of their parents, who need our support; spiritual guides should not undermine parents' rules by their attitudes. While youngsters may verbally or actually rebel against parents' rules, at the same time they crave them and deep down realize that the rules testify to their parents' love and care. Of course, we are talking about *reasonable* rules, and we're not dismissing what we said earlier about the need for flexibility and communication. But the bottom line is that kids *need* structure and guidance.

Helpful adults other than parents may not need to impose many structures, but they still need to offer guidance and support to young people who are often confused and who live in a very complex society. They also can help young people to understand *why* their parents are providing structure and setting limits—out of a love and concern for their child's best interest.

If a parent (and this is rare) insists upon *unreasonable* strictures which only create hostility and alienate a teenager from his or her peers, you, as a friend to both parties, may be able to intercede on a teenager's behalf. Sometimes insecure parents become inflexible in their regulations. With another adult (who also cares about the teenager) to bounce their fears and worries against, a parent might feel less pressured to continue rigidity.

I recall a mother who would never let her son go to the second showing of a movie with his friends because it didn't let out until midnight. Since he was a senior in high school, I called the mother and explained that I felt this was separating her son from his social group as well as building resentment toward her. My suggestion was that she allow him to go but insist that he be home by 12:30 a.m. She felt better talking about the situation with someone, and she better understood the anger her son was harboring.

Of course you tread a tightrope in the teenager-parent relationship. Never tell a parent how to exercise authority (unless you perceive a serious abuse). Much depends on the relationship with the parents, too. And while it is true that some parents are unfortunately threatened by a healthy relationship between a teen and a trusted adult, I honestly believe that most parents are looking for any help and advice they can get in parenting during the stormy years of adolescence.

Chapter
2

You *Can* Be
a Spiritual Guide!

Many people are uncomfortable about being asked to guide another human being in the area of spirituality. Chances are you're asking, "Why me? I'm not perfect! What right do I have?" Sometimes people let a false sense of humility get in the way and conclude it would be *wrong* to try to tell someone else, even a young person, how they should live a Christian life.

But let's look more carefully and more honestly at why we shrink from taking on this role of spiritual guide— whether as a parent or adult friend of a teenager. Often we have two reasons, one good and the other bad.

The good reason is that we feel we are no better or no holier than anyone else. And this is true: Nobody has any more inside track on God than anyone else! This fact should *encourage* us as spiritual guides, not discourage us! (We'll return to this point later.)

The bad reason is that we feel incompetent in the areas of theology and spirituality. We are "just lay people," not priests! "What do I know? I don't have a degree in theology or religious education." This feeling of intellectual inadequacy is a poor reason for hesitating to get involved in guiding a teenager. Theologians are not what young people need. They need friends for life's journey, friends who are just a few steps beyond on the road of experience and wisdom and the struggle to live in God's sight. And that's us—you and me, Christian adults.

If you find that hard to believe, consider these research findings: An extensive survey developed by Search Institute in Minneapolis inquired of Christians of all ages what they were looking for in the people who minister to them (in this case, the clergy). The responses basically boiled down to two major ingredients: (1) an open, affirming, warm attitude toward people; (2) a faith-filled attitude toward life. The ability to teach, counsel, organize, administer, etc., were mentioned secondarily. But notice that the *major* considerations have nothing to do with professional skills or academic background.

Think of yourself. What kind of person do *you* like to go to when you are going through a personal struggle? And think back further. Whom did you seek out for guidance in life or spirituality when you were a teenager? What type of individual adult encouraged you in your own journey?

The second piece of pertinent research was done by Dean R. Hoge and Gregory H. Petrillo and reported in 1978 in the *"Journal for the Scientific Study of Religion"*—a magazine you will never find at your supermarket checkout counter. They surveyed 450 sophomores about why they freely chose to participate in Church youth groups. The first two reasons youngsters gave had to do with parents and peers. The third was that the leader was approachable and sincere and expressed his or her own beliefs with self-assurance.

Notice again, academic credentials have nothing to do with it. Kids respond to someone they feel likes them and is not a phony. It is a "cop-out," therefore, to say you can't work with kids because you're not "qualified"—if you equate qualifications with a certain educational background. If you mean that you don't like teenagers or that you're not open, warm, sincere and affirming, then you may have a point.

So the first "qualification" in becoming a spiritual guide to a youth is *believing in yourself*. You can be helpful to a younger person just by virtue of your personality plus the accumulation of life experiences.

Henri Nouwen, a preacher and writer in the areas of prayer and ministry, defines a spiritual guide this way in his book *Creative Ministry*:

> ...one who attempts to put one's own search for God, with all the moments of pain and joy, despair and hope, at the disposal of those who want to join this search but do not know how.

Kids are often people "who do not know how." Nouwen also says a spiritual guide needs to be a "wounded healer," meaning that we paradoxically "heal" others by revealing our own "woundedness"—an aspect we'll discuss more fully below. For us adults to put our own inner journeys with all the pain and joy "out on the table" for kids to see requires a good deal of vulnerability on our part. Let's add *vulnerability* as the second qualification needed for spiritual ministry with youth.

Anyone who ministers to youth can only awaken faith by sharing his or her own faith. We are all attracted to people in whom we sense an inner freedom which we want for ourselves. By association with "free spirits" we get in touch with a bit of our own inner freedom. It's a contagious sort of phenomenon!

Where does this inner freedom come from? Probably from two things: a deep inner reliance upon God and a healthy self-image. One way to prepare yourself for youth ministry, then, is to grow in your own interior liberation.

Being a Good Listener

One of the greatest gifts we can give to anyone today is *really to listen* to them. Sound counseling theory indicates that people solve their own problems (or at least get a clearer perspective) by talking out loud to another person about the things most on their mind. Good listeners function as mirrors which enable speakers to see themselves more clearly and thereby open doorways to solutions or directions. Young people need good listeners as they speak about *their* issues, *their* concerns and *their* relationship with God.

Here are a few simple tips for good listening:

•Try to pick up the speaker's *feelings*, not just the words. If you sense a youth is angry or anxious or depressed, say so: "You seem pretty down today; is everything OK?" Sometimes teens (and their elders) are unaware of what they are really feeling; other times they are just waiting for somebody else to open them up.

•Try to keep kids focused on what they are telling you without going too far off the track. Sometimes excessive chatter is a defense against talking openly.

•After an event, situation or problem has been explained to you, try to summarize what you think you have just heard. This type of concise summing up assures the speaker you *have* heard what was said.

Once a girl came to me in distress. A teacher had failed her for not turning in a term paper at the end of a course. I sensed that her hostility and turbulence were disproportionate to the event, but I let her keep on talking and vent her anger. She then wanted to stray off the topic and consider the effect of a low grade on her college plans. But I asked her to come back to the issue that led her to talk to me and not to stray off the point.

I tried to sum up both what I had heard her say and

also what I sensed she was feeling: "Sue, I understand that you got a failing grade for this paper, but you have told me that you will still pass the course and that it will have little effect on your overall grade-point average. You have also said that your parents aren't upset with you over this failure. And yet you sound so angry and so full of feelings about this. Could there be something more to it than what you have already told me?"

I'm glad I followed the hunch which developed by listening to her feelings more than to her words. I then learned that she hadn't turned in the paper because she had been hospitalized following a suicide attempt. While she didn't want a failing grade, it seemed better than telling the school authorities the truth. She had not only earned the failing grade, she had also shut herself off from needed concern and support.

We also need to remember that, as much as we may ache for someone, we can never solve another's problems. We all have to take responsibility for our own lives. Don't let teenagers box you into a corner by requesting advice, because then you're responsible if your suggestion fails. Just keep throwing the ball back into the teen's court: "Well, what do *you* think you should do?" This question helps people to get in touch with the solutions that lie within them.

If you really feel you have to offer some concrete advice, try to phrase it as: "Well, this is what *I'd* do—but I'm not you." That way you convey your opinion without directly telling anyone what to do. It is more effective to let people come to their own conclusions and then to concur when they have chosen good values or solutions. (See the junior prom discussion on p. 7.)

Being a 'Wounded Healer'

The quality in an adult which best serves youth is personal openness and vulnerability. Yet this quality is often more easily found in younger people who have not built up the defenses so characteristic of adulthood. How sad! The older we get, the more open, defenseless and honest we should become. We should be freer and freer with each year of life—and yet so often the inverse is true.

Older adults are often concerned with providing a Christian example to the young. This is fine. But we don't provide an example by concealing from teenagers our faults, our dark side, the unredeemed aspects of our personalities. Sheltering teens from our true selves does not help them at all. In fact, it inhibits their growth because it generates reluctance to talk truthfully to us.

If it is good for teenagers to open up about personal problems, doubts and failures, if we preach to them that such openness can bring about real healing and deep community, then they have every right to expect that we will do the same. If we tell them to share with us, we also have to share with them: Justice demands it. We have to be willing to talk to them about our own lives to help them get a handle on living theirs. We even have to share our doubts about the movement of God in our lives. To do so gives them permission also to doubt.

We win respect from kids not by modeling a falsely perfect Christianity, but rather by taking the risks of laying our true selves in front of them and letting them behold us in our entirety. Herein lies the birth of respect.

This explains why adults still in their 20's are so popular with teens. These younger adults are less afraid to share their confusion, their hurt, their emptiness. Because they are not preoccupied with being "role models," they can stand up to the scrutiny of contemporary youth with their extreme concern for authenticity.

A contemporary spirituality demands an unfailing connection between humanity and spirituality. We have to learn that openness to God and to people are one and the same reality. We have to recognize that personal vulnerability freely chosen—so that our brothers and sisters might have life—is a fruit of the Holy Spirit. We have to discover that defenselessness is one of the finest forms of contemporary asceticism. We have to help young people learn that, as Jesus said, it is truth that sets us free.

In his little book *The Wounded Healer*, Henri Nouwen makes the following point:

> A minister is not a doctor whose primary task is to take away pain. Rather, he deepens the pain to a level where it can be shared....When we become aware that we do not have to escape our pains, but that we can mobilize them into a common search for life, those very pains are transformed into signs of hope....This hope in turn leads us far beyond the boundaries of human togetherness to Him who calls His people away from the land of slavery to the land of freedom.
>
> A Christian community is therefore a healing community not because wounds are cured and pains are alleviated, but because wounds and pains become openings or occasions for a new vision. Mutual confession then becomes a mutual deepening of hope, and sharing weakness becomes a reminder to one and all of the coming strength.

Boosting Self-Esteem

St. Bernard of Clairvaux, in his treatise on the love of God, says that the first step is to love yourself. How true this is! If I don't feel lovable it will be very difficult to feel loved by God or by anyone.

This problem of low self-esteem is a serious issue for many teenagers. After surveying 7,000 teenagers, Merton Strommen reported in *The Five Cries of Youth* that self-hatred is a *major* problem for 20 percent of youth and a problem to some degree for many more. Symptoms of self-hatred include problems with peer relationships, academic problems, dating problems, distress over personal faults.

For many kids the chief issue in life is just dealing with their sense of self. When this is the case, your role as a spiritual guide is simply to provide them with warmth and acceptance. If you convey a positive attitude, their own self-love will slowly grow, along with their ability to trust.

This may seem "psychological," not spiritual, to people who grew up in an era that compartmentalized human beings into physical, emotional or spiritual aspects. Now we are realizing we just can't chop ourselves up like that. Our spiritual and our psychological selves are so intertwined that growth in one of those areas is also growth in the other. To the teenagers with low self-esteem for whom we provide affirmation, we are God's emissary, the representative of his love and his acceptance of them. Without us they might never grasp his love for them. What can be more spiritual than that?

C.J. Jung put it this way in *Modern Man in Search of a Soul*:

> The acceptance of oneself is the essence of the moral problem and the epitome of a whole outlook upon life. That I feed the hungry, that I forgive an insult, that I love my enemy in the name of Christ—all these are undoubtedly great virtues. What I do unto the least of my brethren, that I do unto Christ. But what if I should discover that the least amongst them all, the poorest of all the beggars, the most impudent of all the offenders, the very enemy himself, that these are within me, and that I myself stand in need of the alms of my own kindness—that I myself am the enemy who must be loved—what then? As a rule, the Christian's attitude is then reversed; we say to the brother within us "Good for Nothing," and condemn and rage against ourselves. We hide it from the world; we refuse to admit ever having met this least among the lowly in ourselves.

Praying With Teenagers

One beautiful form of spiritual guidance is praying with a teenager. A good time to pray together is at the end of a discussion after you both have had a comfortable exchange.

For one thing, that is easier than at the start of a conversation. It also makes more sense to sum up the issue that has been shared and give it to the Lord for his assistance. For example, when it is time to end a good talk, hold the young person's hand, if you wish, and you can say something like:

> Well, we've talked about a lot today. Let's just take a minute before you go to pray about this matter. I'll start, and if you have anything to add please feel free to—but you can just pray silently to yourself if you prefer.
>
> Dear Lord, take Jamie's heart and flood it with your peace. Give him the strength and courage that he needs to face this problem burdening him. Help him know you are always nearby. Amen.

Praying with someone creates a spiritual bond that is really difficult to describe. But if you try it you will understand what I am talking about. You (and the teenager) may feel awkward at first. Even if you are a little uncomfortable doing this, I would suggest giving it a try. If you take the risk, you will find praying together meaningful and helpful in your spiritual guidance.

But if you are *very* uncomfortable with this suggestion, don't force it. There is no use in making a spiritual guide a nervous wreck—better that you pray *for* your teenager rather than with her or him. If this is more your style, at least mention from time to time that you are in fact including your young friend in your prayers. Just those words offer a real sense of spiritual support. You might even mention what prayer you choose and when you pray it. You might also look for an occasion to send a card to this young person stating your care and your prayers.

Chapter
3

Talking About Prayer

This meditation written by a very normal and not too
"religious" teenager indicates that we ought to take very
seriously the possibility of deep prayer on the part of
teenagers:

> I have found it
> I have seen it
> I have been it
> I was taken by it, and it and I were we
> I was doubtful at first that it wanted me
> I was amazed that it did
> I was overtaken by its strength
> I experienced a fullness that was unexperienceable

I realized that it has always been there
I know that it always will be

It isn't until between the ages of 13 and 17 that the experience of God's peace is *felt* by young people. In other words, it isn't normally until adolescence that a person is likely to have a religious experience on the emotional level.

During the teenage years people begin to develop a relationship with God as a personal confidant to whom they look no longer just for gifts but rather for guidance and support. This is encouraging, because sometimes youth seem so self-centered you wonder if they are capable of letting go of the "Gimme, God" posture of prayer. This means that as ministering adults we can talk about prayer as a relationship with a friend, Jesus—a relationship which has ups and downs and involves all kinds of feelings and needs and desires. Looking at prayer this way can help youngsters to abandon concepts of God as a magic dispenser of gifts.

Prayer can then begin to involve things not easily discussed with other people; it can become a sharing of intimacies. (We should note here that low self-esteem also affects teenagers' prayer. It is intricately connected to the feeling of being unloved by God, with the corollary that God could not possibly listen to *my* prayer.)

For all this deepening understanding of prayer, studies indicate that the major reason adolescents pray is still to ask God for personal benefits. The transition from seeing God as primarily a giver of gifts to relating to him as a personal confidant is gradual. Indeed, we know that many adults are still in this process of growing more spiritually mature.

The early Christian community had to go through the same process. Notice the different conclusions offered in the Gospels to Jesus' discourse on petitionary prayer. Matthew's Jesus says that the heavenly Father will give *good things* to those who ask him (7:11). Luke's Jesus promises the *Holy Spirit* to petitioners (11:13). Perhaps Luke's Gospel represents more mature understanding of what Jesus meant.

Nurturing Growth

But for the spiritual guide the question remains: How are we to deal in everyday life with teenagers' questions about the effectiveness of petitionary prayer? One way is to refer them to Jesus' lesson on persistence in prayer (Luke 11:13). More important is to clarify our own understanding.

God has a personal relationship with those who love him. Further, God so loves people that he is willing to meet them at their own spiritual level. The uneducated old woman who prays for God's intervention in her life will be met by the Lord in the way that she perceives God *should* intervene. God respects her level of maturity and deals with her as a spiritual child. In the same manner the Lord can respond to the teenager in the way in which he or she perceives that God will or should respond. Therefore, delight over concrete answers to prayer is never to be minimized, especially with teens who might be very enthusiastic about God's personal concern for them.

Unlike the old woman, however, teenagers stand challenged by a secular and technological age which poses hard questions about the activity (or lack of activity) of God in human affairs. Spiritual guides have a responsibility to help young people grow in faith so that their spirituality will not desert them in an unbelieving age. This is a delicate task requiring patience, love, prayer and a lot of listening.

To accompany our young people on a journey of faith requires a great deal of personal interaction. Adults need to do a great deal of listening to the teenagers' personal experiences as they work through the turbulent years of growing up. They need to review with them *how* prayer of petition is articulated, offer encouragement, suggest backward glances at their experiences, and help them reshape their prayer in more mature terms.

Schoolwork might be a good place to start. If a boy, for example, tells you he blames God for not helping him pass an exam, you might take advantage of the moment to ask some searching questions:

- Is it really *God's* failure? Did he study as hard as he should have? You can explain that prayer is not a substitute for action; we must work toward human solutions of the same things which we are praying about.
- What is the real need? Is this one test the issue, or is it an attitude toward study that needs a conversion? Does nervousness inhibit him; is it really peace of mind during exams which is his deeper need? Does he need better self-discipline? Can he use this failure to learn about his real human need? God is interested in his total development as a person. Perhaps *that* should be the focus of his next prayer.

By reflecting with adolescents on the nature of their prayer, adults can often make brief remarks which can help expand the horizon of *how* to pray and for *what*.

Prayer does not change God; it changes the one who offers it. Young people might at first hear this truth as an adult's way of skirting the question, "Does God really answer prayer?" But indeed it is not. Persons who have persisted in prayer of petition have experienced this even though they may not be able to articulate the change that has occurred within them. To persist in asking the Lord for help in the face of an "unanswered" prayer is to go on a spiritual adventure. It is to be swept into a deep, profound awareness that the Lord clings so close to us at all times in all situations that we never need to be afraid of anything, including the experience of death. In the words of the psalmist:

> Though a thousand fall at your side,
> ten thousand at your right side,
> near you it shall not come. (Psalm 91:7)

In other words, faith insists we have nothing to fear. If we walk through life trying to be a good person, making decisions about our life as best we can, we should be confident that the Lord will care for us, be close to us, see us through all the difficult things we encounter. The kingdom of God is within us. To discover this reality is to understand Jesus' promise. "Ask and you shall receive, seek and you shall find" (Luke 11:9).

It is this profound discovery which we want for young people. In order to lead them to it, we should challenge some of their childish thinking. More significantly, we must encourage them to plunge deeper and deeper into prayer so that the Spirit can lead them to insights which will sustain them throughout their adult lives. Within this process lies the transition from expecting "good things" to the deeper, more lasting expectation of the "Holy Spirit," God's own unyielding care for us.

Getting Practical

Keep it simple.

Sometimes when we try to explain spirituality or suggest methods of prayer to young people we intimidate them without realizing it. Affirm their own methods of prayer, what works for them. Don't encumber them with a lot of "spiritual vocabulary"; you might make them feel a relationship with the Lord is only for the chosen few.

Simplicity is at the heart of spirituality for a world where we are constantly overstimulated. This doesn't mean we can naively ignore the complexities of our day. It does mean that, amidst the complexity and noise and materialistic values, we need to cling tenaciously to our deepest human and religious values. Simplification implies stripping away what is useless, harmful or needlessly burdensome to our psyches, our pocketbooks, our time, our ambitions. If we are personally involved in such an ongoing conversion process, we needn't be concerned with being models to anyone, for youth automatically respect that which is good and authentic and true.

Discuss the youth's concept of God (or Jesus).

Is God close or far away? Is God warm or cold, concerned or not? Is God a judge or a vague reality, a parent or friend? And where is God—in church, in heaven, in one's heart, in other people? There are really no right or wrong answers to any of these questions, but to ask them helps youth ponder who the Lord is for them personally. You may also unearth some childish notions of God—as a sort of policeman, for example. In this case you can point to God's total acceptance of each of us.

Suggest regular prayer.

Encourage youth to find a specific time to pray each day, even if it is brief. (Five to 10 minutes is sufficient.) Help them to see that any friendship requires spending time with the friend; so too with Jesus. That's what prayer is: developing the friendship.

Encourage them also to have a specific place to pray: perhaps a corner of the bedroom facing a window. Some people find it helpful to create a "prayer corner" or special place to pray with a special mat or rug on which to sit or kneel. (Lying on the bed fosters daydreaming and dozing, so bed is usually not a good place for prayer.)

Lighting a candle or incense also helps create the mood or environment. Playing a mellow song as a preamble to prayer can help teenagers unwind. But ask them to turn the radio or stereo off for at least a few moments of real silence. The prophet Elijah in the Old Testament found that God was not to be found in the loud wind or the earthquake or the fire, but rather in a soft whisper (see 1 Kings 19:12); in other words, to "hear" the Lord requires stillness and silence.

Introduce new prayer forms.

Scripture is an excellent source of spiritual nourishment for young people. The Gospels are more meaningful than theology or doctrine and are helpful because they are so concrete. If a youngster finds it difficult to spend five or 10 minutes a day in prayer without daydreaming, recommend reading a short Gospel section and reflecting on how it applies to his or her personal life. (A list of suggested Gospel passages you can read and discuss together can be found on p. 61.) This type of reflecting on the Gospel (or any other religious writing) is called *meditation*; it involves the intellect, the ability to think and reflect.

Another form of prayer more alien to our hectic Western society is *contemplation*. It is alien because, first of all, it requires that we be totally relaxed and slowed down, that we turn all our interior motors off. Our society is so geared to activity and achievement that it is very hard for most of us to just stop and be still.

The most important thing to turn off in contemplation is the activity of the mind: memory, imagination, the thought process. Contemplation is quite different from meditation, which relies on the mind's activity. Contemplation is a simple attempt to be still and know God—the deepest form of communication with God because it is the experience of love itself. On a human level meditation resembles two friends in conversation, while contemplation resembles two people who know each other so well that they can just gaze at each other without words and feel intense love.

Contemplative experiences cannot be forced. Sometimes they just happen—for example, when we are overcome by the roaring of the sea or the beauty of a sunset: a natural contemplative experience. The effect of nature is so profound that we suspend all our thought processes, if only for a few moments. This can also happen in prayer sometimes—we can be so overwhelmed by an experience of God's love that we just bask in that feeling for a few moments without having any thoughts.

In the last century there lived in France a holy priest named St. Jean Marie Vianney. People came from miles around to go to him for confession because of his wisdom and sanctity. A legend has it that each day the priest noticed a man just sitting in a pew and staring at the altar. Thinking that the old man was desirous of going to confession but fearful to do so, St. Jean Marie approached him one day: "I notice you sitting in this church every day. Would you like to go to confession?"

"No thank you," said the old man, pointing to the crucifix on the altar. "I just sit here and look at him and he looks back to me." This is what we mean by contemplation.

Generally this deeper form of prayer is a gift given to those who have been faithful for some time to daily meditation. I would not recommend it right away to a teen unless he or she is experienced in prayer.

Recommend asceticism.

That harsh-sounding word comes from a Greek word meaning "to exercise." It refers not to prayer itself but to preparation for serious prayer.

Asceticism implies the self-control to shut the door and be removed for at least a short while from the noisy confusion of the world. It means the self-discipline to turn off the radio and perhaps take the phone off the hook for 15 minutes so prayer can proceed undisturbed. Asceticism means that we choose to sit upright rather than stretch out on a couch in order to be fully attentive to communication with the Lord. Asceticism also means we spend the amount of time we have promised ourselves, no matter how many distractions come our way.

Diet and physical exercise are also ascetic practices related to prayer. It's hard to focus on our communication on a purely "spiritual" level if we have a too-full stomach or are feeling the effects of caffeine or sugar or some other substance. The more balanced and nutritious our diet, the better tone our bodies will have and the more we will feel prepared to turn to prayer. So too with exercise. Exercise tunes our bodies and clears our minds so that we are able more easily to turn to God in prayer. In fact, the best time to pray is often after a good physical workout, transforming the natural "high" of the activity into an opportunity to commune with God.

Encourage journal-keeping.

A good habit for anyone intent on a life of prayer is to keep a daily journal of the Spirit's movements experienced in mind and heart. A journal helps us focus on our relationship with the Lord and will indicate areas where growth is needed or the directions in which the Lord is calling. A "nothing book" with blank pages (sold in gift shops) makes a good journal. If your youngster is willing to share what he or she has written (or at least part of it), it can serve as a good springboard to your session together.

What is written in the journal probably isn't as important as *that* it is used. It's just another form of slowing down; it takes self-discipline to write in a journal every day. Young people who are growing and changing so quickly can trace their progress over the past year or even the past few months by rereading the pages of the spiritual journal.

Define genuine religious experience.

Sometimes certain phenomena are mistaken by youth as "spiritual experiences"—the peace induced by marijuana, for example. Here are a few criteria for discerning a real spiritual experience. If a young person describes something that you don't feel is genuinely religious, check out your hunch against these points adapted from *The Practice of Spiritual Direction*, by William A. Barry and William J. Connolly:

- Does it *seem* like a religious experience? Does it compare to previous experiences of which you are more certain? Is it consistent with what you know of God or Jesus, or does it just seem too strange or contrived or "far out" to you?
- Is it honest? Does it come out of true feelings? (This may be very difficult to sort out with adolescents because they have such a jumble of intense feelings.)
- Is it characterized by a genuine sense of peace? Does it bring calm to the spirit?
- Are *all* the fruits of the Spirit (see Gal 5:22-23) present

as a unified whole? In other words, is the effect love, joy, peace, patience, self-control, etc.?

Help prayer flow from feelings.

It is important always to pray from the feelings we are presently experiencing: This is something many adults need to learn, too. There is no right mood for prayer, nor should we artificially create one. If you're angry, tell God. He can take it, even if you're mad at him. If you're sad or down, then pray from those feelings; if you're peaceful or upbeat, pray from those. When we pray from our "gut," we are genuinely praying as well as seeking liberation from any negative moods. Previous generations had a tendency to block out negative feelings from prayer. Through psychology we have learned that repressing feelings, not admitting them even to ourselves is not healthy. And spiritual writers today tell us that prayer requires being honest with God (who knows our hearts anyway!).

Don't be afraid of doubt.

In a technological age where we can do so many things ourselves (reach the moon, build an artificial heart), God's primacy can easily be overshadowed. Our young people are growing up in a culture that relies very little upon the Lord; this is the society which is the backdrop of their religious faith. Coupled with this is another phenomenon: The crisis of faith which used to be common in early adulthood often occurs now during late adolescence. Does God exist? This question usually rises from the more sensitive, reflective young person.

As a spiritual guide, don't overreact to this crisis. It is quite normal (even if you never experienced it yourself). It is more common now that faith has so few cultural supports, but spiritual writers have talked about this over the ages as a crisis which occurs in many souls. Faith, we must always remember, is a gift from God—not something that we can manufacture ourselves.

If young people are truly seeking the meaning of life

and ultimate reality, we just have to wait quietly and patiently until they are gifted by a new and more profound awareness of Jesus Christ in their lives. If they honestly confront their own inner emptiness, they will eventually discover that only the Lord can fill them up. If they honestly confront their own unhappiness, they will eventually discover the Christian paradox that happiness comes from unselfish concern about the happiness of others. And if they honestly confront their own mortality, they will eventually discover that only in Christ is there victory over death.

Studies show that most children eventually return to the religious values with which they were raised. They may drift for a while away from the faith community, from participation in the Eucharist and other forms of prayer. They may even do this in a rebellious way. The best thing we adults can do during this time is to be good sounding boards and listen to their doubts and concerns. We also can be patient with their alienation and not take it personally. And—most important of all—we can pray for them.

Talk about Sunday liturgy.

Young teenagers often oppose attendance at Mass as a way of testing parental limits. Discerning the difference between this "testing" and an older youth or young adult in a real crisis of faith can be "thorny." Pressuring the latter to attend could harm spiritual growth rather than help it. Below are some possible directions to take with the question (see the Bibliography for further help):

- No matter how much you disagree, try to listen *patiently* to a teenager's objection. Feeling heard is, in all probability, half the issue. In the area of faith, we need to show deep respect for another's viewpoint even if the other is young. We can't ever lose sight of the fact that Jesus' entire message is an invitation, not a command—and we need to reflect his attitude.
- Offer a challenge if you feel it appropriate. Ask what *the teenager* contributes to improve parish liturgy. Has he sought out a more meaningful liturgy at another

parish? If she wants to worship God on her own on the sabbath, how does she plan to do that? Remember that harshness may alienate someone totally; be very sensitive in this area.

- Explore parish opportunities for teenagers to work on the liturgy with other people their age to render it more meaningful to them. Would that be of help in deriving more fulfillment from attendance?
- Realize that most spiritual formation occurs in the family. Most youngsters learn religious practices in the home and, if they reject them for a time, there is a high probability that they will readopt them in the future. If you are not the parent of the teenager you are guiding, there may be very little you can effect regarding Sunday church attendance. Leave it to the Lord and don't be personally distressed and aggravated.
- Share your reasons for attending Mass. The Eucharist is one of the most precious gifts Jesus left us. Your own appreciation of that gift will say much more to young people than your words. When the rich young man refused to follow him (Mark 10:17-23), Jesus did not coerce him to a Christian life-style. He accepted the man as he was. We must always remember that Jesus is our model for inviting young men and women to follow him.

Chapter
4

Talking About Morality

Morality is a word often misunderstood. Many people see it as synonymous with a certain standard of sexual behavior; others relate it to honesty in business dealings. Both these interpretations are very limited in scope. Perhaps newer words are needed to express a broader range of right and wrong behavior.

Moral and *immoral* refer to inner attitudes as well as to external behavior. The feeling of love in our hearts or the intellectual idea of love is not enough. Love must be translated from feeling and thinking into concrete action in order to be real and credible. Love is not only an interior disposition, it is action with and for others. It is precisely this action which is the living out of Christianity and following Jesus Christ's way of life.

Many popular songs have beautiful lyrics about the nature of love. But if love remains within us like the lyrics of a song and never gets translated into action, then our love is empty and meaningless. As Scripture puts it:

> My brothers, what good is it to profess faith without practicing it? Such faith has no power to save one, has it? If a brother or sister has nothing to wear and no food for the day, and you say to them, "Good-bye and good luck! Keep warm and well fed," but do not meet their bodily needs, what good is that? So it is with the faith that does nothing in practice. It is thoroughly lifeless.
>
> (James 2:14-17)

Action and behavior are the *proof* of loving, beyond words and thoughts and feelings. A person can be said to live a "moral" life if he or she is really trying to put love (and all that the word encompasses) into practice.

Immorality is basically a refusal to care about others; it is selfishness. It can take the form of unloving sexual behavior or dishonesty in business dealings, but it has a thousand other faces, such as failure to share one's material goods or failure to communicate within the family.

Forming Conscience

Conscience, as some of us were taught, is the "little voice" within us which distinguishes right from wrong, moral from immoral. Guilt is its by-product when we have chosen a wrong attitude or action.

As we mature, our understanding of conscience needs to mature. A more adult way to understand this psychological/spiritual dimension of our personalities is to think of conscience as a "developed sensitivity" or a "willing awareness." It means that we keep ourselves open and allow the gospel message of love to flood our entire being. It means that we keep before our mind's eye Jesus' command to love our neighbor as ourselves. When we choose not to block this commandment from our conscious awareness and to allow the needs of others to affect us at an emotionally healthy level, we begin to develop a mature Christian conscience.

A mature Christian conscience means that we try to see the world with the eyes of Jesus Christ and keep alive within us an attitude of compassion and gentleness. This is what it means to live a moral life.

Conscience must be distinguished from scrupulosity, which is a minutely critical examination of all our actions which, in the end, blocks all action. For example, a person so afraid of talking about other people *sinfully* may scrupulously avoid all conversation about anyone, even when it would be beneficial for all parties for another person to be the object of discussion. The person who has a fundamental Christian perspective on love of neighbor will normally operate out of that, however, and will sense when the conversation is becoming slanderous or cruel. That loving attitude will dictate when the conversation needs to be quickly concluded.

To help young people form their consciences or make a moral choice, suggest to them the following five steps:

1) Gather all the information or data about the issue being decided.
2) Get advice from someone with more life experience who can be *objective* about the choices.
3) Carefully consider Christian tradition: Does Scripture say anything about this choice? Does Church teaching?
4) Seriously pray over the choice to be made.
5) Listen to the heart, one's honest "gut" feelings.

A person who actually follows through very seriously on these five steps and is willing to accept the consequences and responsibility of the choice is indeed "free to follow his or her conscience." And personal conscience *is* our highest norm for moral decision making! But the process of rightly forming conscience is far more complicated than what is suggested by the attitude: "If I think it's right, it's OK."

Recognizing Personal Sin

We can summarize morality as "loving behavior." To relate the word *sin* to this approach, go back to its original Greek meaning: "to miss the mark." We can put that another way: not to be our best self. Love is a constant struggle, and many times we fail to act in the most loving way because of our own laziness or selfishness or weakness. We miss the mark of doing the loving thing; we fail to be the best self we can be.

In no way does this approach to sin minimize our wrongdoing. But it does keep the focus on our behavior and our struggle to be good people. It doesn't say that since we have sinned, we are evil people. Therefore, a good self-image is compatible with the daily struggle to grow and live in spite of the fact that we fail so often.

Theologians today tend to look upon sin not so much as a specific act but as the "drift," or pattern, of a person's life. For example, a husband who neglects his relationship with his wife over a long period of time, who fails to communicate and share with her, may eventually become involved with another woman. The drift this man's life has taken away from his wife is his sin, not just the act of adultery. Serious sin is when the wrong one does becomes so much a part of a life that it affects the entire being and turns a person away from God.

We can also look at sin as a form of as saying no. A line from the musical *Hair* goes, "Easy to be hard, easy to say no." We talk about *committing* sin; but another perspective—and perhaps a more significant one—is to look at sin as refusing to do the good that we could do, as *saying no* to love: sin by omission. For example, it is sinful to steal from a poor person; it is also sinful for affluent people never to think or care about the poor and never to lift a finger to help.

Commission and omission are the classic categories of sin. But modern awareness adds another dimension which could be called *submission.* By this we mean the unreflective tendency to conform to the norms of peers, national values and the mores of our society. Some people seem to live like robots, always going along with whatever "the crowd" thinks and does. This refusal to take personal responsibility for our life-styles and to make choices for ourselves about what is right or wrong can be another aspect of sin.

Being Aware of Social Sin

Still another category of sin can be called *transmission.* What we choose to do in this complex society (the food we eat, the products we buy, how we invest our money, how we participate in government) affects people all over the world. While we cannot be expected to master the complexities of world economics, we cannot ignore our connectedness to other people.

We are involved in moral decisions in our collective lives, in the structures of our society. In the days of slavery, for example, many slaves and their masters were Christian. To many of the latter, slavery seemed moral as long as the slaves were treated kindly. Today we look back and say that society was caught in a sinful structure without being aware of it. The very idea of slavery goes against Christ's teaching that we are all equal before God. The equality and dignity which each person deserves is called justice; any social structure that is unjust is sinful or morally wrong.

Racism is a sinful structure in our society; judging a person by skin color is unjust. Sexism—holding that either sex is superior—is also unjust, as is prejudice based on nationality, religion, sexual preference. And so when we examine our consciences to see if we have sinned or refused to love in our personal lives, we also need to ask ourselves if we are a willing part of sinful structures in society. For we contribute to injustice by our own actions, or by not speaking up when we can.

Dealing With Guilt

Guilt is the product of conscience; it flows from sensitivity to our failures. Guilt is often characterized by a depressed feeling—a feeling of dislike for our sinfulness and sometimes even an intense dislike for ourselves.

The first thing we need to understand about guilt is that *feelings* have no morality; they are neither good nor bad. It is not wrong to have sexual feelings, angry feelings, fed-up feelings. The wrong comes when we *express* our feelings inappropriately. But the feelings themselves should not give us a sense of guilt. For instance, the *appropriate* expression of anger should not arouse guilt. Anger is a healthy emotion; but buried inside, it can do serious damage.

Consider the story of Frank, whose alcoholic father was both physically and verbally abusive toward him. The physical abuse waned as Frank grew into adolescence and became physically stronger. But he was still outraged with his father. The treatment he had received bothered him, as well as the way his father treated his mother.

When Frank became very involved in the leadership of his parish youth group, he began to believe that hatred and revenge are un-Christian and sinful. And yet his heart was filled with such rage over his father's conduct that he often had fantasies about actually killing or hurting the man. Frank's dilemma was having one set of philosophical values and a completely opposite set of emotions. He felt that his hatred for his father separated him from Jesus' favor. But Frank's real challenge was to work through his deep anger with a counselor or trusted adult who could teach him legitimate ways to confront his father and to express his hostility in appropriate and healthy ways.

While we need to deal with our feelings to grow emotionally (and spiritually), we must also recognize that the feelings themselves are not sinful. Young people need to be taught this distinction and also to be challenged to deal with their emotions.

If we sin and act unlovingly it is healthy to feel shame, remorse and irritation with ourselves. Out of these feelings can come resolutions to change or repair our behavior and continue the struggle for growth. This is healthy guilt. *Unhealthy* guilt lets us wallow in our emotions, feel self-hatred, get depressed. We indulge these feelings as a substitute for making concrete resolutions and taking steps to change our behavior. Guilt, then, can be useful, but it should lead to action.

Responding to Critical Issues

Sexuality

The strong emergence of sexual feelings and the ensuing confusion is part of what we all remember about being a teenager. It's tough for youth today to live out Christian sexual values because the culture at large offers so little support.

A new study of young adolescents completed by Search Institute indicates that almost 20 percent of Christian young people have had intercourse before they enter high school! And a recent Gallup poll reports that 50 percent of American teenagers have sexual relations before graduating from high school. Teenage pregnancy is alarmingly on the rise. Also, we are increasingly aware that a good number of youth—perhaps 10 percent—are sorting out their sexual identities and deciding that they are homosexuals. Traditional concepts of masculinity and femininity are being forcefully challenged in many quarters. In short, we are still in the midst of a cultural sexual revolution which impacts the Church.

If a teenager brings up a sexual question, issue or problem with you, consider yourself quite trusted. It's probably the riskiest area a youngster could discuss with an adult. Despite their seeming sophistication, young people harbor many questions and fears in the area of sexuality. Here are few suggestions to help you address sexual issues:

- Try to remain calm, unshocked and open when teenagers begin to discuss sex. They are asking for help, so ask some probing questions if they seem to have trouble saying what they want to say. (Being comfortable with your *own* sexuality is of course the best preparation for a conversation of this nature.)
- Be accepting. Recall the discussion of sin (on p. 44). Help alleviate unhealthy guilt by talking about God's wholehearted acceptance of us despite our failings.
- Give them (or get them, if need be) whatever specific and necessary information they request. They could even need a referral for a specific kind of counseling or a medical exam.
- Be firm in upholding traditional values. The cherished viewpoint that sexual activity should be reserved to marriage safeguards commitment to another and to the children of the union.
- Be realistic with regard to adolescent sexual behavior. (This is easier when you are more emotionally detached from a teenager than a parent.) You have to retain a sort of "pastoral realism." In the process of growth and development, young people may very well have sex—and learn painfully some of the lessons that premature involvement can teach. Do not be too harsh on their mistakes, but simultaneously challenge them to the high standards of moral behavior which faith holds.

Death

One of the most common fantasies in the adolescent mind is the anticipation of how others will react to his or her own death. A certain bittersweet pleasure is often derived from anticipating the belated recognition of good qualities.

Some adolescents think of themselves as infinite, while others dwell on their mortality. One 16-year-old girl wrote: "The more I read about life's splendor, the more I see its tragedy: the fleetingness of time, the ugliness of age, the certainty of death. The inevitability is always on my mind. Time is my slow executioner. When I see large crowds at the beach or at a ball game I think to myself: 'Who among them is going to die first and who last? How many of them will be dead next year? Five years from now? Ten years from now?' I feel like crying out 'How can you enjoy life when you know death is around the corner?'" Of course, alcohol and drug abuse, automobile accidents and teenage suicides have left few young people strangers to the reality of death.

The death of a parent puts a great stress on a teenager, as does the death of a teenage friend. The experience of loss, however, is often a real source of growth and movement to a higher level of faith at any age if it is met with honesty and compassion. Never avoid the topic if a youth needs to discuss it. Don't allow your own fears of mortality to stand in the way.

Violence

We are witnessing today a real rise in violence within the youth subculture. It's a very scary reality. Violence is often a quite acceptable part of the dating relationship. This is partly so because teenagers take their cues from the rest of society which still sees violence as an acceptable means of resolving conflict. Many psychologists also feel that low self-esteem results in lack of respect for other people. As adults we need to encourage young people to accept the challenge of honest communication as the only healthy means of negotiating solutions to conflict.

Fear

In additon to fears carried from childhood, new ones loom large on the teenage horizon—mostly involving social interaction. Fears of speaking out in class, failing examinations and being disapproved of by peers become extremely pronounced during the teen years. The two major problems among both boys and girls are "making something of myself" and "the mistakes I've made."

The spiritual guide can greatly alleviate anxiety by an

accepting manner. Being a good listener offers tremendous support to a young person. Also, of course, there is prayer. Remind frightened young people that the Lord has invited us to come to him whenever we are heavily burdened.

But during times of distress *group* prayer often works better for adolescents than individual prayer. Because they incline toward introspection, teenagers' private prayer can easily turn into a period of mulling over problems, whereas group prayer can be a real source of strength and encouragement. It is therefore helpful at times for the spiritual guide to pray with the adolescent. Even a normally hesitant teenager thinks of turning to God in the case of emergency.

Contemporary studies suggest that the threat of nuclear destruction is a significant factor in shaping personality, even in the very young. This is something most of the adult world grew up without—and so is often overlooked or misunderstood by adults. Young people realize that adults are unable to protect them from this ultimate threat to life. The seeming inevitability of nuclear destruction can render every endeavor and commitment tenuous to the teenager. Uncertainty about whether they will even have a future has a subtle impact upon teenagers' viewpoints regarding putting off pleasure (indulgence in sex, drugs) and investing energies in long-range enterprises (studies, relationships). This is, of course, very difficult to document, but psychologists increasingly testify to the growing impact of the constant threat of nuclear destruction.

Suffering

One of the most difficult experiences for the teenager comes with the struggle to understand the why of suffering. Many teenagers suffer because of worry about situations over which they're powerless. They have not come to appreciate the comforting thought that it does not add a single cubit to a person's stature to worry over anything, or that today's worries are sufficient because there's nothing that we can do about tomorrow anyway.

Kevin at age 17 wrote this: "When I think of suffering, I think of mental suffering rather than a physical one. It seems that the suffering that I have remembered in my life was more mental suffering. When my parents divorced I think I suffered. Two people I loved very much didn't seem to love each other. The pain and suffering I felt inside seemed much worse than any physical suffering I can ever remember experiencing."

A conversation with Kevin a year or so after his parents' divorce revealed that he was counseling a friend who was undergoing similar suffering. Kevin at that time remarked to his peer that there are certain situations in life over which we have no control; what we have to learn to do is accept them rather than worry why they are the way they are. Kevin advanced a giant step during that year.

Many teenagers simply find life's situations difficult to accept and churn with the question "Why?" They have not yet dealt with the lack of control we have over this life.

Sources of suffering for the teenager are generally worries about school or family. Appeal to the opposite sex and how one's physical maturing compares to peers are also of great concern. Adolescents need to succeed in some way, or else feelings of inadequacy—real or imagined—can be sources of great suffering.

Trust

Adolescents, like all of us, are striving to trust more deeply in God; they also are searching for trustworthy people with whom to share their deepest human experiences. The astute spiritual guide is, of course, aware that his or her own relationship with the adolescent must be one of trust in order to encourage trust in the Lord and in other people. Many adolescents feel that the problems they are experiencing are uniquely theirs. A wise adult will encourage young people to talk about life experiences with a peer or a group of peers in order to assure themselves that they are pretty much like everybody else. Teenage retreats which encourage group sharing can be tremendously helpful to adolescents struggling with the issue of trust.

Drinking and Drugs

Despite the variance in national surveys, it is realistic to assume that 50 to 60 percent of teenagers indulge in drugs—and not just occasionally. Most high school parties today include beer and wine if not harder drinks or other drugs. Even teenagers who don't drink are confronted by the choice at most of the parties they attend.

It's incumbent on parents and school personnel today to be aware of drugs like pot and cocaine and others as well ("uppers," "downers," hallucinogens, etc.). Naivete is inexcusable. We adults have a responsibility to be aware of the very prevalent and very dangerous elements of the youth culture today. Most adults, however, are usually quicker to detect alcohol abuse than the use of such unfamiliar drugs as pot or cocaine or speed.

Marijuana (or pot, or weed) is widely used among teens, although there are indications that it is declining a little bit in popularity among youth. Pot often reddens the eyes or gives them a glazed look. It usually causes a mood change such as withdrawal, lethargy or giddiness. To "get stoned" means to smoke enough pot to feel emotionally numbed to the point that nothing troubles you. Marijuana use can make some people slightly paranoid (especially if they fear being detected); it can also lead to hunger cravings.

Youth are quick to point out that alcohol use by the adult community has more deleterious physical effects than marijuana. This may be true, but on the other hand there still is no agreement on the long-range effects of marijuana use.

Cocaine is a drug whose use is very difficult to detect. It creates a subtle euphoria or peacefulness, yet the user loses no control. It is often "cut," or mixed with, "speed" (stimulants), resulting in hyperactivity or talkativeness. Cocaine is very expensive; its users can be reduced to deceit or theft in order to obtain it. Cocaine is usually snorted up a straw into a nostril. It is white and looks like baking powder.

Here is a variety of perspectives important for adults who are close to teenagers:

- A particular drug is not usually used in isolation. Young people experiment with combinations of drugs and often mix alcohol with some other drug.
- Teenagers have to know they will not be totally rejected if caught under the influence of some drug. Parents often overreact to drug use out of fear, stereotypes or ignorance about the exact nature of the substance. This type of "hysterical overreaction" is not helpful because it distances adults from the experience of the young. Kids know a great deal about drugs and many of their parents do not. To discover a small quantity of marijuana in a teen's trousers should be a cause of concern and confrontation, but it should not cause a parent to lose control or make all kinds of accusations. This is where, as a third party, you may be able to serve as a "bridge" between parent and teenager and create an atmosphere where this serious topic can be discussed calmly, rationally and constructively. The best way to deal with drugs is to be educated about them.
- Involvement with drugs (including alcohol) *is* potentially addictive. While some younger teens may still try drugs in a spirit of youthful flirtation or as a rebellious experimentation in defiance of adult authority, this is not the usual scenario. Primarily, most youth use alcohol and/or marijuana regularly for the same reason adults once reported: to escape the pressures of their lives. As one teenager living in a difficult home situation remarked: "I smoke a joint every morning before breakfast just to take the sharp edge off of my day." This is a dangerous state of affairs: The vulnerability of youth coupled with the confusion of adolescence makes alcohol or drug involvement potentially addicting. To discover drugs as a coping

mechanism at such an impressionable point in life can quickly lead down the road of self-destruction.

As adults we must first be role models, particularly with respect to alcohol, the drug of adult society. Only "do as I do" teaches lessons to the young—not "do as I say." While we don't want to communicate a puritanical and totally negative attitude toward indulgence, we need to communicate the *limited* value of alcohol. We also need to encourage youth to discover natural "highs," the sense of exhilaration in becoming a skilled athlete, developing talents to their fullest potential, achieving academically, working hard for a sense of satisfaction.

We also should help them discover the deeper sense of fulfillment that comes from Christian dedication to the needs of the suffering in society as well as the joy and peace that comes from intimacy with Jesus Christ in prayer. Again, it's more important that they see us living in this fashion than that we preach to them about it: The way we deal with *our* pressures will teach them volumes about how to deal with theirs.

Coping With Divorce

A tragic figure among contemporary youth is the "psychological orphan." This is the teenager who either feels a lack of parental trust or chronically experiences the household as a place of conflict. Constant fighting between parents can be extremely damaging to a young person. A lot of research suggests that, despite the pain involved, it is better for the teenager if parents separate if there is no other way to restore peace and harmony to a household.

Parents' separation or divorce is of course a traumatic crisis for a child. It is probably hardest on teenagers: Just as they are struggling with self-definition, their primary role models shift ground. This can really complicate the process of identity formation which we discussed earlier (see Chapter One).

Guilt is also a problem. Often adolescents have an irrational but very real feeling that they themselves were the cause of the divorce. Another problem is deciding which parent is due allegiance. Parents often (overtly or subtly) press the teenager for loyalty. This dynamic puts a tremendous strain upon young people.

Here are some guidelines for working with a teenager whose parents are undergoing divorce:

- Young people need to talk about the painful experience with an adult *who is not their parent.* Parents are usually so caught up in their own hurt and anger, confusion and fear, that they lack the objectivity to be truly helpful to their own son or daughter.
- Encourage the parents to communicate with their teenager about what is going on. They need to explain why the separation is occurring. They each need to be respectful of the young person's feelings for the other parent.
- Young people need to be encouraged to talk with peers. In their circle of friends there probably is someone who has also experienced divorce. Many schools have group counseling or support groups.
- Teenagers need to know they are not to blame for the divorce. They may need your help as an adult to convince them of this. They need to be given a *lot* of time to adjust to stepparents or new parent models. You may be able to help parents be patient with this process and not yield to their own anxiety to "make things work." As teenagers advance in years and emerge into young adulthood, their decisions about the amount of time to spend with each parent, holiday plans, and so on deserve respect. Your objectivity as a third party can be very helpful.
- Teenagers need to remain involved in their own projects, education and emotional development, and not be totally swept up by the difficulties at home.

Helping in a Crisis

Teenagers in our day are less and less protected. Mass media make them immediately aware of society's problems. They feel pressure to perform well athletically, academically and socially—even from the preteen years! They must juggle time and schedules just like adults. Symptoms of increased stress include more drinking and doing drugs, more sexual acting out, a higher suicide rate, anorexia and other eating disorders, more runaways.

Parents often worry about the unstructured sphere of a teenager's life, the hours when a young person is out on his or her own. At the same time, despite these fears, parents are unwilling to invest much time with their teenage children. One new study reports that the average father spends just five minutes a day interacting with his teenager!

Given these dynamics, we shouldn't be surprised that teenagers are often in crisis situations. And so how does the spiritual guide, the "amateur counselor," respond to such events?

First, let's define a "crisis": an event (or accumulation of events) where normal, everyday coping mechanisms break down. To respond, we suggest the following:

1) Respond directly, using common sense and trusting your human instincts.
2) Remain as calm as possible.
3) Try not to become overinvolved emotionally with the problem—withhold yourself deliberately.
4) Explore *precisely what happened.*
5) Stabilize the crisis by doing the first thing that needs to be done depending on the specifics of the situation (see below).
6) Refer the young person swiftly to the appropriate person or agency who can give necessary help.

Below are suggested "first things that need to be done" in certain situations.

Drug overdose: Get immediate medical help; don't use your own remedies first.

Rape: Get emergency medical help. Deal very sensitively with the young woman; be aware of the guilt she is feeling. Encourage her to make even a small decision about what to do immediately in order to help her begin to regain a sense of control.

Sexual abuse: Believe the young person. Be as calm and gentle as possible and encourage the young person to define the situation accurately (starting with earlier experiences can be less threatening).

Bad news: If you are called on to break bad news, do so sensitively but in a slightly detached way. Whether the news comes *through* you or *to* you from the teen, help the youth sustain the impact of the blow. Let him or her work through the predictable stages of shame, anger or grief.

Family fights: Help the youngster define precisely what issue brought about the crisis. In other words, try to provide some *minimal* perspective.

Suicide: Always take a suicide threat seriously (eight out of 10 suicide victims give a warning). Don't be afraid to ask a depressed teenager if he or she has ever considered suicide. (You won't put the idea in anyone's head.) If the answer is yes, ask further if a *method* and *time* are in mind. The more specific these are, the more dangerous the situation. If you seriously suspect that a youth is potentially suicidal, tell everyone who should know, everyone who can possibly help. Don't get caught in a confidentiality trap here.

Conclusion

A Final Challenge

In closing, I would like to challenge *you*, the spiritual guide, to examine your own image of Jesus, the image which you undoubtedly will convey to your teenager. To do so I would like to quote Dr. Michael Warren, a real pioneer in youth ministry. This is taken from his speech, "New Stage in Weekend Retreats for Teenagers," published in *Origins* (June 21, 1986):

> I have been concerned about the vision or portrait of Jesus being presented in many different programs for middle-class youth. This Jesus tends to be a middle-class Jesus, representing the dominant concerns of the moderately well-off and privileged. The dominant concern of the middle-class tends to be greater

comfort, and thus the middle-class Jesus is presented as the one who comforts. Overlooked is the Jesus who not only comforted but who also confronted and challenged, Jesus the upsetter. The middle-class Jesus is not the "man for others"; the middle-class Jesus is the "man *for us*."

If there is any challenge offered by such a presentation of Jesus, it is the challenge of accepting him as a sign of God's love for us. Obviously it is essential to understand Jesus as God-with-us and as God's special gift to us. Accepting Jesus as God's love embodied is an important first step on the road to discipleship. Yet, to go no further is to remain with a middle-class and ultimately false image of Jesus.

The Gospels remind us in many ways that Jesus offers us not so much the Jesus-hug as a call for ourselves to embrace the poor and the weak and those who do not fit. In the Gospels Jesus continually calls attention, not to himself, but to the social situations that needed to be changed and to the people who suffered in these social situations, the poor.

The most exciting thing about being a spiritual guide to a teenager is that it is an opportunity to reexplore and rejuvenate our own faith. Young people have a wonderful gift for keeping us enlivened, challenged and authentic. Undoubtedly their own questions and issues will touch the churnings of your own heart and soul. Try not to be afraid of this, but rather look at it as an adventure in further Christian maturity. As we said at the outset, it's a journey *together*. As your teenager grows, so will you.

Gospel Passages
for Reflection and Discussion

Passages	Suggested Focus
Matthew 5:38-48	Who are your enemies? How do you treat them?
Matthew 6:1-9	Do you ever brag or feel "spiritually superior"?
Matthew 6:24-34	Do you trust God?
Matthew 7:13-14	What do you need to eliminate from your life to walk the "narrow way"?
Matthew 10:26-33	Are you ever ashamed of your religion?
Matthew 10:37-39	What form of unselfishness do you feel called to? What's holding you back?
Matthew 13:1-23	What kind of soil are you?
Matthew 19:16-24	Are riches your obstacle to God? If not, what is?
Matthew 24:37-44	Do you feel spiritually "prepared" to meet God?
Matthew 25:31-46	When is the last time you fed the hungry, clothed the naked or visited the sick?
Luke 10:25-36	Do you ever pass people by?
Luke 11:5-13	Do you persist in prayer?
Luke 12:13-32	Is there anything you hoard? Do you share generously?

Luke 14:12-14	Do you do things for people who could never repay you?
John 3:1-8	Do you feel the need for a spiritual "rebirth"?
John 4:1-26	When do you think you have failed to recognize Jesus?
John 6:35-40	Do you appreciate the gift of the Eucharist? Do you receive Communion frequently?
John 8:1-11	Are you ever tempted to think of yourself as better than others and put them down?
John 10:1-14	Do you rely on Jesus to take care of you?
John 15:1-7	Do Jesus' words "remain" in you?

Bibliography

For the Adult Guide

Images of God

Kushner, Harold S. *When Bad Things Happen to Good People.* Shocken Books, 1981.

Phillips, J. B. *Your God Is Too Small.* MacMillan, 1971.

On Ministry

Bourdon, Mary. "The Spiritual Direction of the Teenager," *Spiritual Life,* Summer 1982, pp. 92-101.

Nouwen, Henri. *The Wounded Healer.* Image, 1979.

Wensing, Michael. *Ministering to Youth.* Alba House, 1982.

DiGiacomo, James, and Edward Wakin. *Understanding Teenagers.* Argus, 1983.

On Teenagers

Shelton, Charles. *Adolescent Spirituality.* Loyola University Press, 1983.

On Crises

Kennedy, Eugene. *Crisis Counseling.* Continuum, 1981.

Yudkin, Marcia. "When Kids Think the Unthinkable," *Psychology Today,* April, 1984, pp. 18-25.

Books for Youth

Daily Meditation Books

Link, Mark. *Breakaway.* Argus, 1980.

Moore, Joseph. *Monday Morning Jesus.* Paulist, 1984. (While especially for youth who have experienced a weekend retreat, these daily meditations can apply to any teenager intent upon developing spirituality.)

Sexuality

Cooney, Nancy H. *Sex, Sexuality and You.* W. C. Brown, 1979.

Reichert, Richard. *Sexuality and Dating.* St. Mary's Press, 1981.

Self-Image

Powell, John. *Why Am I Afraid to Love?* Argus, 1967.

Powell, John. *Why Am I Afraid to Tell You Who I Am?* Argus, 1969.

Feelings/Expressing Emotion

Simon, Sidney. *Caring, Feeling, Touching.* Argus, 1976.

Spirituality

Jones-Prendergast, Kevin. *Letters to God From Teenagers.* St. Anthony Messenger Press, 1979.

Searching

Hesse, Hermann. *Siddhartha.* Bantam, 1951. (Due to the mature subject matter, I would only recommend this to older adolescents.)

Morality

Smith, Joanmarie. *Morality Made Simple (But Not Easy).* Argus, 1982.

A Meeting for Sponsors

This meeting (one and a half to two hours in length) is designed to ease sponsors into their role and to provide an overview of the whole preparation process.

For this meeting you will need: nametags; sound equipment; a slide projector (optional); pencils and paper or a mimeographed handout with the Reflection questions and writing space; a copy of *When a Teenager Chooses You* for each sponsor.

Greeting

The first thing to keep in mind is that the people attending this meeting may be feeling uncomfortable or insecure about being a sponsor. In addition, they may not know anyone else at the meeting. It's important, therefore, to help people to feel comfortable as quickly as possible. Some suggestions are:

- Greet people as they enter.
- Ask sponsors to fill out a nametag.
- Offer coffee or soft drinks as people arrive.
- Begin the meeting on time. Delaying the starting time causes great discomfort for people already ill at ease.

Introductory Exercise

If the group is small (15 people or less) place their chairs in a circle. With a larger crowd, divide the participants into groups of four or five. Ask the sponsors to:

- state their names,
- state their candidates' names,

- tell how they feel about being asked to be sponsors. (The articulation this question requires will help dispel any anxiety about being at this meeting.)

Reflection

Ask the sponsors to reflect for five or 10 minutes on their own adolescence and to recall the places and people they perceived as holy. To help them do this, play a recorded song which reflects the changes we go through over life's journey. A few suggestions are: (1) "Only the Heart Can See" (Dan Fogelberg and Emmylou Harris), (2) "Try to Remember" (from soundtrack of *The Fantasticks*), (3) "Forever Young" (Rod Stewart). To enhance the mood, you may choose 12 to 30 slides to accompany the lyrics – pictures of people from infancy to old age – to help the sponsors reflect on the passage of time.

Then ask the folks to answer the following questions individually. (The questions may be listed on a prepared handout sheet. If you wish, replay the song softly as the sponsors complete the exercise.)

1) What place seemed holiest or most sacred to you when you were young?
2) What person from your childhood or adolescence stands out in your memory as a holy person?
3) What qualities did you admire in that person?

After five or 10 minutes, invite the sponsors to share some of their responses with their group.

Instruction

Take 15 to 20 minutes to introduce the ideas in Chapter Two of this book. Don't pass out the books until the end of the meeting, otherwise the sponsors will be tempted to page through the book. Ask them to read the rest of the book on their own.

Break

Presentation

It is very helpful to prospective sponsors to hear from a recently confirmed *articulate* young person who can help the sponsors crawl into the psyche of an adolescent preparing for Confirmation. Points in this five- to 10-minute presentation should include:

- a brief description of the "world," the concerns of young adolescents,
- some thoughts about what Confirmation may mean (or not mean) to the candidates,
- advice on being good listeners and cautions against feeling strongly the need to direct a young person's life,
- a short witness on this young person's own experience of the sacrament and the benefit of his or her own sponsor relationship.

Overview of Upcoming Candidate Meetings

The specifics of the next 10- to 20-minute segment depend on what kind of sponsor-candidate interaction you expect. Below are three models:

1) a four-hour mini-retreat for sponsors and candidates,
2) a loosely structured one-on-one program for sponsors and candidates using the suggested Gospel texts on pp. 61-62,
3) a four-part, structured one-on-one program for sponsors and candidates.

Question Period

Take five or 10 minutes to encourage sponsors to direct their questions to you, the parish priest or the young speaker.

Closing Prayer

Spirit of God,
Spirit of Jesus present among us tonight [today],
give us the grace and wisdom we need
in order to bring our young people closer to you.
Help us never to forget that it is your Spirit
who instructs the human heart,
who transcends all our human weaknesses and failures.
Prepare the hearts of our young people to receive you afresh
in the Sacrament of Confirmation. Amen.

A Mini-Retreat for Sponsors and Candidates

This mini-retreat is a three- to four-hour afternoon or evening program for sponsors and candidates. Choose an environment which is as warm and inviting as possible. If you must use a church hall, try to enhance the environment by bringing in table or floor lamps rather than using harsh overhead lights. Don't use tables except to do written exercises (tables create barriers between people).

For the closing prayer you might wish to use your church sanctuary if it's warm and carpeted. Set up folding chairs in a circle or horseshoe; invite those who wish to sit on the floor.

You will need these materials: nametags and markers; pens or pencils; candles and matches; a crucifix; index cards; paper or mimeographed sheets for Exercises One and Two.

Ice-Breaker

The purpose of this 10-minute ice-breaker is simply to help people feel more at ease. Set up the meeting area with back-to-back pairs of chairs. As people arrive, give them nametags, an index card and a pen or pencil. Ask sponsor and candidate to sit with their backs to each other.

Begin the meeting by asking sponsors and candidates to write on the index card, without looking at the other, their best estimate of:

1) the color of their sponsor's/candidate's eyes,
2) their sponsor's/candidate's shoe size,
3) where their sponsor/candidate would most like to go on vacation,
4) their sponsor's/candidate's favorite TV show,

5) a celebrity their sponsor/candidate admires.

When they are finished, ask them to write on the back of the index card two statements about *themselves:* one true and one false.

Then invite the sponsors and candidates to turn their chairs toward each other and share their answers with each other and to correct each other's answers.

Next invite each pair to join with another pair (preferably people they do not know). Ask them to introduce each other by describing their partners with the correct answers to the five questions.

Have each group member read both the true and false statements about themselves. Group members should then guess which statement is which.

Exercise One

Retaining groups of four, pass out paper and give sponsors and candidates five minutes to complete the following sentences privately:

1) An area of my life in which I feel challenged to grow spiritually is:
2) One of the most difficult things about faith or religion for me is:

Presentation One

Ask a teenager (perhaps recently confirmed) and an adult (perhaps someone who has been a sponsor) each to make a 10- to 15-minute "witness talk," sharing their responses to these two questions. These sharings should really be *sharings* – not instructional, philosophical or "preachy." They should also be as candid and open as possible; they should include details and personal stories.

Sharing

After the speakers' presentations, invite the groups of four to spend 15 minutes sharing their responses to the first exercise. No one should be pressured to reveal his or her answers; each person should share at a comfortable level.

Break

Presentation Two

Another young person and another adult each make a 10- to 15-minute witness talk based on the questions in Exercise Two (below).

The same qualities listed in Presentation One should mark these sharings. Be sure that both sexes are represented. The four speakers should not be all males or all females.

Exercise Two

Ask sponsors and candidates to take five minutes to answer the following questions:

1) On a scale from one (very distant) to 10 (very close), what is the quality of your current relationship with Jesus?
2) What obstacles (if any) keep you separated from Jesus?
3) What is your hope for your future relationship with Jesus or for your experience of the Sacrament of Confirmation?

Sharing

Give the groups of four 20 to 30 minutes to share their
responses and also to respond to what other group
members say. Again, no one should be pressured to reveal
his or her answers; each person should feel comfortable
with the sharing.

Optional Audiovisual

Before moving to prayer, you may wish to show a short (15-
to 30-minute) audiovisual. Maintain the reflective mood; an
instructional video on sacraments or the role of the
sponsor at this juncture would contrast too sharply with
the personal sharing of the day.

    The suggestions below each deal with adult-teen
relationships (although not specifically with the Sacrament
of Confirmation). Most are available on either 16 mm. film
or VHS tape.

1) *Pardon and Peace* (Franciscan Communications,
   1229 South Santee St., Los Angeles, CA 90015). The
   story of a runaway boy and the forgiveness of his
   family (11 minutes).
2) *Bridges* (Franciscan Communications, 1229 South
   Santee St., Los Angeles, CA 90015). A story of the
   hurt and the healing that occurs between
   generations (23 minutes; videotape only).
3) *17 Going on Nowhere* (Insight-Paulist Productions,
   P.O. Box 1057, Pacific Palisades, CA 90272). The
   story of communication between a father and son
   (28 minutes).
4) *Rocco's Star* (Insight-Paulist Productions, P.O. Box
   1057, Pacific Palisades, CA 90272). A film focusing
   on a parent's need to let his son make his own
   future life choices (27 minutes).
5) *The Shopping Bag Lady* (Mass Media Ministries,
   2116 North Charles St., Baltimore, MD 21218). A story

of a teenage girl's discovery of the human behind the exterior of a street person (21 minutes).

Prayer Service

An atmosphere conducive to prayer is crucial to this 30- to 45-minute service. If you are using a hall, dim the lights and put a candle, a crucifix and a Bible on a small table or on the floor in the center of the circle. If you are in a church, sit in a circle on the sanctuary carpet or form a ring of chairs around the altar instead of sitting in the pews. Also dim the lights.

As people enter, play a song on tape or ask them to sing an opening song. An excellent mood setter appropriate to Confirmation is the Taizé chant "Veni, Sancte Spiritus" from either *Taizé Cantate* or *Taizé in Rome* (tape or record from GIA Publications, 7404 South Mason Ave., Chicago, IL 60638). Invite the group simply to repeat the refrain, "Veni, Sancte Spiritus."

Reading

Ask someone to read aloud 2 Thessalonians 2:13 – 3:5 from the Bible in the center of the circle.

Passing of the Crucifix

Take the crucifix from the center of the circle. Say that you are going to pass it around the group. Ask that each one take it and while gazing at it pray briefly either aloud or in the privacy of one's own heart. Model the prayer aloud by beginning the circle with yourself or someone else who is willing to pray aloud.

After the crucifix has gone around the circle, return it to its place in the center.

Litany of the Holy Spirit

The response is "Come, Holy Spirit."

Leader: Into our world weary of war,
        (response)
        Into our nation needy of guidance,
        (response)
        Into our families longing for healing,
        (response)
        Into our parish praying for unity,
        (response)
        Into our hearts seeking your grace,
        (response)

The response is "Spirit, give us strength."

Leader: To be witnesses to Jesus,
        (response)
        Not to fear the disapproval of others,
        (response)
        To be faithful when it's difficult,
        (response)
        To be prophets for our day,
        (response)

The response is "Refresh us, Lord."

Leader: With your rejuvenating grace,
        (response)
        With your body and blood,
        (response)
        With your tenderness and mercy,
        (response)
        With your comfort and guidance,
        (response)
        With your Spirit which ever renews,
        (response)

Concluding Prayer. Come, Holy Spirit, and renew the suffering face of this earth. Bless our parish community as we eagerly await your coming again into our midst at the celebration of Confirmation. Keep us all free from harm as we expectantly await your outpouring upon us. Amen.

An Unstructured One-on-One Sponsor-Candidate Program

Whatever the duration of the sponsor-candidate program, the 20 Gospel Passages for Reflection and Discussion (pp. 61-62) can serve as a basis for the conversations between sponsor and candidate. The sponsor should choose an appropriate number of the Gospel selections which he or she feels will elicit the most discussion.

Here are some basic guidelines for these sponsor-candidate meetings:

1) Plan to spend 20 to 45 minutes on each meeting.
2) Choose a mutually agreeable time and a place where quiet conversation will be possible.
3) Begin the meeting by reading the Gospel passage and the commentary aloud.
4) Encourage sponsors to share as much as candidates. Sponsors' role is to be co-journeyers and sharers of the faith, not teachers or catechists.
5) If possible, conclude each meeting with spontaneous prayer.

A Structured Four-Week One-on-One Sponsor-Candidate Program

The following material includes suggestions for four distinct one-on-one meetings between sponsor and candidate using Scripture as a springboard. The following directives apply to each meeting:

1) Meet in a quiet place for 45 to 60 minutes.
2) Begin by reading the appropriate Scripture text aloud.
3) Ask both sponsor and candidate to complete the Exercise in writing and then to share their responses with each other.
4) Close each meeting by joining hands and praying briefly in silence, praying spontaneously or saying the Lord's Prayer together.

Meeting One

Scripture

> How blest are the poor in spirit;
> the reign of God is theirs. (Matthew 5:3)

Commentary

There are two ways of being poor. In this early chapter of his Gospel, Matthew is not talking about the poverty that comes from having no money or from living in destitute conditions. The type of poverty that Matthew says brings true happiness is a different kind indeed, for we all know that to be without material possessions is no guarantee of a joyous life. Perhaps a better word than *poverty* in this passage would be *dependency.*

We may not often think about experiences of being dependent, yet we have these experiences all the time. For example, if it were not for our alarm clock or our mother or father we would not have awakened this morning on time. Do we ever stop to realize that small area of dependency in our lives? Do we stop to think how dependent we are on the food that we eat each day to keep our bodies in good health? In our modern society we take for granted so many things, like electricity, the telephone and the television set, that we are often not even aware of our reliance on them.

In this brief line from his Gospel, Matthew is talking about a type of *spiritual* dependency. Perhaps the key to this passage is *knowing* how dependent we are: Happy are those who *know* that they are poor. Some of us delude ourselves by thinking we are not dependent on anything or anyone – either for material goods or for more important things. Do we ever stop to realize that we are?

Exercise: **Recognizing Dependency**

Complete the following sentences:

1) Three *healthy* dependencies in my life are:
2) One *unhealthy* dependency in my life is:
3) I depend upon Jesus to help me in my struggles __ percent of the time.

Meeting Two

Scripture

You have heard the commandment, "An eye for an eye, a tooth for a tooth." But what I say to you is: offer no resistance to injury. When a person slaps you on the right cheek, turn and offer him the other. If anyone wants to go to law over your shirt, hand him your coat as well. Should anyone force you into service for one mile, go with him two miles. Give to the man who begs

from you. Do not turn your back on the borrower.
(Matthew 5:38-42)

Commentary

Under Jewish law one person could sue another for stealing a shirt, which was a longer garment than our shirts of today. In these examples Jesus is rejecting an ancient Near Eastern custom of revenge. But we know that the Gospel was written for all people and holds a message for us here and now.

Not many of us are going to do the things mentioned in this passage. There are all sorts of ways, however, that we can translate these examples into our own lives. What about lending money repeatedly to a friend? What about running an errand for someone twice in the same day? And what about doing something or going somewhere with a friend, even if we don't particularly care to, simply to allow the friend to express his or her preference?

This is a very difficult passage, both in terms of understanding what it means and in the challenge it presents. You can see from this brief reading that to be a good Christian requires more than just going to church on Sunday morning.

Exercise: **The Call to Kindness**

1) Name a person in your life to whom you are sometimes (or often) unkind.
2) Name an area in your family life where you could be more kind.
3) Name one reason for your most usual lack of kindness.
4) Name an area in your friendships where you could be more kind.
5) Name an area in your life where you feel Jesus would like you to "go an extra mile" of kindness.
6) Name a resolution you can make for tomorrow (a specific act of kindness you could perform).

Meeting Three

Scripture

[Jesus] proposed still another parable: "The reign of God is like a mustard seed which someone took and sowed in his field. It is the smallest seed of all, yet when full-grown it is the largest of all plants. It becomes so big a shrub that the birds of the sky come and build their nests in its branches." (Matthew 13:31-32)

Commentary

Patience is not a common virtue in the United States. All you need to do is to stand and watch people at a McDonald's on a Friday evening to realize this fact. We are used to instant coffee, instant pudding, instant-on TV sets and automatic tellers. On an airplane or a bus that has arrived at its destination, disembarking passengers press forward as if restlessness and rushing will get them out the door more quickly.

Patience does not come easily in the American culture. The patient woman will often find herself standing alone in a crowd that is rushing about in a frenzy. The patient man will often be accused for his seeming inactivity. And yet, if we are to meet Christ in a closer way, we shall have to prepare our hearts quietly, carefully. To expect an immediate, deep relationship with the Lord is to make the mistake which our frantic culture urges upon us.

Spiritual growth demands emotional growth, a great deal of human experience, much time and prayer. Growth in human relationships – emotional growth – is a long process. Spiritual growth is also a long process, one that entails fidelity to prayer and to worship. The fruit of that fidelity is the coming of Jesus into our lives at an ever deeper level.

Exercise: **Jesus and Me**

1) Indicate the quality of your current relationship with Jesus on a scale from one (very distant) to 10 (very close).
2) List two obstacles which keep you from Jesus.
3) Name an area about your relationship with Jesus that confuses you.
4) Name one way you know you could grow closer to Jesus.

Meeting Four

Scripture

Immediately afterward, while dismissing the crowds, Jesus insisted that his disciples get into the boat and precede him to the other side. When he had sent them away, he went up on the mountain by himself to pray, remaining there alone as evening drew on. Meanwhile the boat, already several hundred yards out from the shore, was being tossed about in the waves raised by strong headwinds.

At about three in the morning, he came walking toward them on the lake. When the disciples saw him walking on the water, they were terrified. "It is a ghost!" they said, and in their fear they began to cry out. Jesus hastened to reassure them: "Get hold of yourselves! It is I. Do not be afraid!"

Peter spoke up and said, "Lord, if it is really you, tell me to come to you across the water." "Come!" he said. So Peter got out of the boat and began to walk on the water, moving toward Jesus. But when he perceived how strong the wind was, becoming frightened, he began to sink and cried out, "Lord, save me!"

Jesus at once stretched out his hand and caught him. "How little faith you have!" he exclaimed. "Why did you falter?"

Once they had climbed into the boat, the wind died down. Those who were in the boat showed him reverence, declaring, "Beyond doubt you are the Son of God!" (Matthew 14:22-33)

Commentary

Let's start by saying that God does not usually contradict the forces of nature he has established. Therefore, this miracle must be considered a very special one, meant to teach a universal lesson. The lesson, of course, is that of *trust*. Peter's problem, basically, was that he didn't dare put his entire confidence in Jesus' invitation to come to him.

The question this raises to us is: How willing are we to put our trust in other people? Do we really believe that people care about us, that they enjoy being with us, that they love us? Or do we doubt other people and always ask ourselves questions about their sincerity and motivation?

If we distrust others, it is usually because we have had some bad experiences along the way. Perhaps we once told a secret to someone and that person betrayed us. Maybe we once thought someone was our friend and that person hurt us. After bad experiences like this, the human temptation is to crawl into a shell. But this leads to loneliness and isolation and increases our misery.

It is true that people sometimes hurt us, even people we trust. But we must be careful about two things. First, when people are inconsiderate toward us, it is sometimes because they are having personal problems. They may be in poor health. They may be jealous of something we have done. This is why ongoing communication is so important between friends and families. By talking things out, we usually realize that we are still very lovable.

The second thing we must be careful about is our reaction toward life after we really have been rejected, after an experience of misplaced trust. Just because one person really has let us down, we cannot let that interfere with establishing new relationships.

Exercise: **Trust Barometer**

1) On a scale of one (not at all) to 10 (all the time), rate how much you trust yourself, your friends, your parents, Jesus.
2) In what area in your life do you wish you could develop more trust?
3) When is it difficult for you to trust Jesus?
4) Do you see a way you could grow in trust?